The Martyrs of Matanzas

The Huguenot Cross

The Martyrs of Matanzas

by

Sara Ballenger

"And they loved not their lives unto death..."
(Revelation 12:11)

America's First Martyrs: The Martyrs of Matanzas
©Copyright 1999 - Sara Ballenger
Encouraging Word Publishing Services
Printed by Accent Digital Publishing
2932 Churn Creek Rd.
Redding, CA 96002
(530)223-0202
http://www.accentdigitalpublishing.com

ISBN 978-1-60445-062-0

All rights reserved. This book is protected by the copyright laws of the United States of America. This book may not be cpied or reprinted for commercial gain or profit. The use of short quotations or occasional page copying for personal or group study is permitted and encouraged. Permission will be granted upon request.

Cover by Morgan Fisher: Accent Digital Publishing
Art work by Stanley Meltzoff

DEDICATION

This edition of this small volume is being published as a memorial to the lives of the Martyrs of Matanzas, 445 years after they perished at Ft. Caroline, Florida. It is dedicated to the many intercessors who have fought to possess the birthright of this nation.

"And they loved not their lives unto death..."

(Revelation 12:11)

September 20, 2010

Contents

Dedication	5
Prologue	9
Introduction	11
The Huguenot Community	15
The Destruction Of Fort Caroline	21
The Martyrs Of Matanzas	27
Timeline Of Events	32

AMERICAE

VIRGINIA

1607
JAMESTOWNE

CAROLINA

OCEANUS
ATLANTICUS

SAVANNAH
1733

St AUGUSTINE
1565

FLORIDAE

GOLFO
DE

PROLOGUE

"To everything there is a season, and a time for every purpose unto heaven." (Eccl. 3:1)

The time has come to issue another edition of this little volume, The Martyrs of Matanzas. As we do so, our hearts are filled with joy, knowing that since we first released this book in May, 1999, more and more intercessors across the United States are, indeed beginning to understand that our nation's modern history began not with the English, but with the Spanish—and the French. Certainly, before Matanzas, there were forays into this land by various missionaries, explorers, and conquistadors. But there had been no permanent village established in our land, until September 8, 1565, when a Spanish armada, led by Captain General Pedro Menendez de Aviles, founded St. Augustine (now in Florida)—the oldest city in America. Within a matter of days, these fearless and fearsome Spanish soldiers found their way to a sandy inlet a few miles south of their new outpost. What happened next IS the story of Matanzas—the story of "America's Buried Treasure." This tale is difficult to recount due to its tragic nature; yet it is one which must be told from a Kingdom perspective, for our Lord had His hand in the lives of His people all along....

As you begin reading The Martyrs of Matanzas, we will "take you by the hand" and share with you the unusual way this story first came to light—in the halls of the United States Congress in January, 1999. We will share the results of our research with you, as well as a work of corporate intercession that followed a few months later. We then leave this information in your hands, to do with as our Lord would direct. In my own case, as a descendant of a French Huguenot family, the Ammonets, I have been deeply moved to actually stand on the sands of Matanzas inlet, and to imagine what these precious saints must have endured in persecution. I offered identificational repentance on the land in April, 1999, and several times since then. Each time, the weeping in my own spirit is hard to describe, but "joy cometh in the morning."

In this hour, in the United States, the persecution against those who hold our faith seems to be growing more pronounced by the day. Soon, we too may have to draw directly from the wellspring of our unknown Huguenot pioneers, who faced the sword without fear on behalf of the uncompromised gospel of our Lord Jesus Christ. May the flame of faith that they carried across that vast ocean 444 years ago be yet rekindled in our day, and may revival fires burn across our land in these tumultuous times!

Sara C. Ballenger
Capitol Hill Prayer Partners
Herndon, Virginia

August 29, 2008

INTRODUCTION

AMERICA'S BURIED TREASURE

What follows is a piece of history, hidden from our eyes until now, that reveals spiritual treasures when studied carefully. You see, the European history of the United States did not begin with the establishment of a fort at Jamestown in 1607, nor did it begin with the founding of Plymouth by the pilgrims in 1620. No, the story of this land really began one-half century earlier ... on a sandy inlet simply called Matanzas.

Discovering the Map

How did we discover this missing piece of American history? The clue came early in 1999 in the halls of the United States Congress. Two of us had completed our work of intercession on the Hill and were preparing to return home, when we came upon a corridor in a corner of the House of Representatives that was new to us. As we gazed upon the murals covering the ceiling of the hallway, we noticed that this corridor seemed to be devoted to the earliest parts of American history. There were paintings of a Viking ship, Native Americans waiting to pounce on a herd of buffalo, and—most interesting of all—a map showing the East Coast of North America, our earliest days.

Studying this map, we saw Plymouth (1620), Jamestown (1607) and Savannah (1733). Almost ready to turn-away, my eye caught one more city on the map: St. Augustine (1565). 1565! Suddenly I realized that this date was older than that of Jamestown... older by almost half a century. Why was this city shown on that map? I asked my prayer partner, Marie, "Do you know anything about St. Augustine?"

"No," she answered, as we both pondered the date on that map.

The Martyrs of Matanzas

"But, isn't St. Augustine still a city in Florida?" I asked. (I knew that Marie had family in Florida, so perhaps she would know the answer to this question, too.)

"Yes," she stated. "One of our children lives not too far away from St. Augustine."

"Did you know that this city was founded before Jamestown?"

"No, I didn't," said Marie, adding that this was probably something we should look into.

Before we moved on, I noticed another detail on the mural: the illustrator had drawn a large, strong fortress near St. Augustine, but it was positioned somewhere out in the Atlantic Ocean. The fortress had an unusual shape: the fort, its moat and landscape, formed an eight-sided figure. We left the site mystified, determined to learn more about the history of this part of northern Florida when we got home.

Discovering the History

Studying my encyclopedia that evening, I found that Pedro Menendez de Aviles of Spain founded St. Augustine on Sept. 8, 1565. Apparently, the King of Spain, Philip II, wanted to establish a colony in this territory, which Spain had claimed since the early part of that century. Unlike the Lost Colony of North Carolina, (which had been established by Sir Walter Raleigh in 1585 and then mysteriously disappeared), St. Augustine never perished, but has been in existence continuously since its founding in 1565. Therefore. St Augustine; Florida. is the oldest European city in what is now the United States of America. This information was news to us, but we soon learned that there were more secrets to that map.

While I was studying my encyclopedia, my friend was studying hers. Her source was older than mine and provided more detail. She learned the truth about WHY this city was founded: Menendez had set foot on the land with express orders from the King of Spain to find and drive out a colony of French settlers that had been established nearly one year earlier. But these were not "ordinary" settlers. These men and women were Huguenots; French Calvinists who had broken away from the Catholic Church in order to worship the Lord without interference from Rome. In the mind of King Philip II of Spain, these colonists were heretics whose revolutionary ideas were absolutely dangerous to the established power structure of his state. To remove these colonists from the land, the king appointed a man who shared his passion for seeing this heresy destroyed, Captain General Pedro Menendez de Aviles. In the fall of 1565, General Menendez carried out his orders, in a series of massacres, and the Huguenot colony was obliterated. Spain then controlled the Atlantic Coast, from the present Florida Keys up to what is now Southeastern Carolina, until 1819.

What continued to baffle us was why we, both college graduates with graduate degrees in education, no less, had never heard about any of this. We had always been led to believe that our country had been founded at Jamestown and that our basic system of government had grown out of the Mayflower Compact of 1620. For the most part, the nation had basically been built upon a British foundation and the British had simply annexed the Spanish territories later on.

Well, we were wrong. We were wrong about the facts of our earliest national history, and we were wrong about the foundation of this nation.

While our civil system of government did emerge from our beginnings at Plymouth, the story of this Huguenot colony—largely hidden from view until now—reveals a much deeper foundation. In the pages that follow, we will share this truth with you, because this part of America's heritage is really a major source of our strength as a people.

The Huguenot Cross

The Huguenot Cross is a symbol of religious loyalty - a religion so strong that it did not even fear the stake. Descendants of the Huguenots are not allowed to forget their origins nor to consider their religion as being something superficial.

The Huguenot Cross is not only beautiful and symbolic, but possesses the added charm afforded by the romance of history and tradition. It recalls a period of valor, constancy, faithfulness and loyalty to truth. It is becoming more and more a sign among the descendants of the Huguenots throughout the entire world.

The four Gospels are symbolized by a Maltese Cross formed by a four petalled 'Lily of France'

The eight Beatitudes are represented by rounded points

The twelve Apostles are signified by four Fleur-de-lis, with three petals each

The open space is heart-shaped

The Holy Ghost is signified by a pendant dove

Acknowledgement: Huguenot Society of South Africa
For more information visit:
http://www.geocities.com/hugenoteblad/x-eng.htm

Chapter One

THE HUGUENOT COMMUNITY

The story of the founding of St. Augustine really begins one year earlier, in 1564, when an expedition of French Huguenots established a colony in present-day Jacksonville, Florida. In order to understand the lifestyle of this people group, we must study their ways in their native France. In the fifteenth century, a group of men in France began to break away from the traditional teachings of Rome, choosing instead to study the Bible for themselves and to be led directly by the Spirit of the Lord in their day-to-day lives.

The Catholic Church, then the official church of France, was greatly threatened by this move, which it interpreted as weakening its absolute authority over the people. As a result, Huguenots were harassed continuously and some even faced death because of their faith. Indeed, the name "Huguenot," as applied to the dissenters by the Church of Rome, is supposed to have been derived from "Hugeon," a word used in Touraine to signify persons who walk at night.[1] For over 100 years, the only safe place for the Huguenots to worship had been inside dark caves where, huddled together, these men and women studied the Word "in Spirit and in truth"

Plans for a New Colony

By the middle of the sixteenth century, some Huguenots, under the leadership of Gaspard de Coligny, Admiral of France and a prominent Huguenot himself, began to seek a way of escape from this persecuted lifestyle. As a man of great wealth, Gaspard de Coligny had favor in the court of nine-year-old King Charles IX and his influential mother, Catherine de Medici. In 1560 these persecuted saints had a breakthrough: Coligny worked out a plan with the royal family that would allow the Huguenots to explore the New World and to eventually establish a colony there, if the colonists would promise to search the area for the rumored silver and gold once they had arrived.

The Martyrs of Matanzas

Thus, in 1562, Admiral Coligny dispatched a fearless military man, Jean Ribault, with three ships for the purpose of exploring the coast of La Florida to find land suitable for colonization. On May 1, 1562, Ribault and his company set foot in present day Jacksonville at St. John's Bluff on what they then dubbed the River of May (now called the St. John's River). Having established a marker and uttered a prayer to dedicate this work to the Lord, they then explored the coast, eventually returning to France to give a report to their patron.

Two years later, Coligny sent another man, Rene de Laudonniere, to the new land to head up the new colony. Laudonniere was given three ships to fill with supplies for this venture and was allowed three hundred people on the voyage. In order to fill the ships, Laudonniere included a few passengers in the group who were not Huguenots: six Catholics, some Moors (who followed Islam) and a few Frenchmen who had been released from prison. The remaining majority were Huguenot believers. On April 22, 1564, Laudonniere left France with the three ships to build a life for the Huguenots in the new world. Six weeks later, they had crossed the ocean, sailed up the coast and spotted Ribault's marker on the land. The voyage ended and success awaited these hopeful few.

Upon landing on June 30, 1564, Laudonniere led his group in expressing the following prayer of thanksgiving to God for their safe passage:

> *On the morrow about the break of day, I commanded a trumpet to be sounded, that being assembled we might give God thankes for our favourable and happie arrival. Then wee sang a Psalme of thanksgiving unto God, beseeching him that it would please him of his grace to continue his accustomed goodnesse toward his poore servaunts, and ayde us in all our enterprises, that all might turne to his glory and the advancement of our King.* 2

The Huguenot Community

The prayer ended, and every man began to take courage.

The Colonists' First Encounter with the Native American Timucuan Tribe

"On their first arrival at St. Johns Bluffs, Laudonniere, with a detachment of twelve soldiers, reconnoitered the land. Three Indian chiefs with more than 400 of their tribesmen met them and made signs of friendship. The Indians, who had learned to hate and fear the Spaniards, welcomed the French. It also appeared that the natives not only recalled the visit of Ribault but had made a god of him, and the column he had erected had become their idol. Despite later difficulties, the French leader managed to retain the friendship and help of Chief Saturiba and of many other Indian leaders who probably admired his shrewdness, a quality which they coveted themselves."[3]

The Establishment of Fort Caroline

The French named their community La Caroline, after their king, Charles IX. With the help of their new Indian friends, the French began building a triangular shaped fort, which was fortified with walls, bulwarks, the cannon they had brought with them from France, and a moat. An impressive gate was constructed, bearing the coat of arms of France, and of their patron, Admiral de Coligny. Then La Caroline was re-named Fort Caroline—a name it retains to this day.

"Inside the fort, buildings housed the munitions. Some houses were erected within the fortifications, but many others were built outside its protective walls of timber and sand. Sentinels were stationed by the fort and on nearby St. Johns Bluff to watch for and protect the settlers from surprise attack from unfriendly Indians or Spanish soldiers."[4]

The Martyrs of Matanzas
Life in the Colony

At first, life was very good at Fort Caroline. The Timucuan Indians were friendly neighbors; the land produced good crops; and the waters of the St. Johns River teemed with fish. More important to these Huguenot settlers, however, was the fact that they were now free to worship the Lord as they chose. Every day at noon, a bell was rung in the middle of the colony, and its residents were called to a worship service. Surely, their main goal in coming to the New World—the freedom to worship—had now been achieved.

Problems in the Colony

However, as time passed, a series of problems began to develop which, if unresolved, threatened the very existence of the community. The biggest need was food. Laudonniere had been led to believe that France would continue to send supplies for the community so that they would be free to search for gold. That promise did not materialize and eventually, some of the French began raiding the Timucuans' storehouses for food. Skirmishes soon developed between the two groups. To make matters worse, the Moors (who were not of the God-fearing Huguenot group) began to run rampant in the Timucuan camps, particularly looking for women. Laudonniere found it so difficult to keep this entire group under control that in August of 1565, the colonists decided to marshal their remaining resources and head back to France on the three ships that were still anchored in the river.

For two weeks, the ships sat slack in the water, waiting for a wind to come up in order to put out to sea. But on August 28, 1565, there appeared on the horizon a cause for great rejoicing: seven ships flying the flag of France had entered the south end of the bay. Laudonniere's group was wild with joy. It looked like Fort Caroline would survive, after all. This miracle occurred because Admiral de Coligny, made aware of the colonists' plight from stories told by pirates, had once again dispatched Jean Ribault to lead seven large

The Huguenot Community

ships and six hundred Huguenots to Fort Caroline. When Ribault joined this group, he immediately took command of the fort. The future looked very good indeed for this hearty band—except for one thing. Troubles of another sort would soon befall this happy group... troubles that even now were heading to their shores.

---

1 Website: "http://pagesprodigy.comvrh2l0a/ressegui/htm" Watson, Colonel James Tompkins, The Journal of the American History. Experiences of the French Huguenots in America: The Kings' Refugees. 1908

2 Website: "http://www.plimoth.org/librarv/Thanksgiving/altemat.htm" Plimouth-on-the- Web. Claimants for the First Thanksgiving, pp. 1-2

3 Charles E. Bennett, Fort Caroline and Its Leader, The University Press of Florida, Gainesville, FL; 1976, pp. 22,23.

4 Ibid., pp. 19, 20.

Fort Caroline

Chapter Two

THE DESTRUCTION OF FORT CAROLINE

The Chase Begins

While they were rejoicing, Jean Ribault, Rene de Laudonniere and their ecstatic troops were unaware of other activity going on not far from Fort Caroline. It was activity that would shortly cost them dearly. You see, in the spring of that year, spies from France had brought news to the King of Spain that a band of French Huguenots had explored land in the Spanish Territory of La Florida and that they had actually established a colony there.

King Philip II was furious. Not only was this an affront to the sovereignty of Spain, it also would greatly endanger his trading ships that sailed along the coast. But the worst part was that these renegades were HUGUENOTS—that vile group of heretics that had dared to defy the authority of the Church of Rome! No, this was very bad news indeed and it must be dealt with immediately and thoroughly.

King Philip II knew exactly whom to appoint to rid Florida of the French: Captain General Pedro Menendez de Aviles, a passionate follower of the Cross of Rome and the ablest of Spain's naval commanders and military leaders. Menendez was instructed to find the French settlers in Spanish Florida and drive them out by any means necessary.

On June 29, 1565, Menendez set sail from Cadiz, Spain with 700 men to search out and destroy the Huguenot colony in New Spain. After sailing across the ocean all summer, Menendez arrived in La Florida. To the fanfare of trumpets, the firing of cannon, and the shouts of 700 colonists, Pedro Menendez de Aviles stepped ashore on September 8, 1565. As the flags flapped briskly in the breeze, Father Francisco Lopez celebrated a solemn Mass of thanksgiving. Menendez and his company knelt to kiss the cross and to receive the priest's blessing. Menendez then proclaimed that the land belonged to King Philip II of Spain. St. Augustine was established.[1] Menendez named the city in honor of St. Augustus, whose feast day it was.

The Massacre at Fort Caroline

During the next two weeks, the Spanish colonists worked to create a habitable village. In the meantime, working with the natives, Menendez sent scouts up the coast to determine the location of Fort Caroline. The following is quoted from Fort Caroline and its Leader, by Charles E. Bennett.

> On September 16, 1565, Menendez led his men north, guided by a French traitor named Francis Jean. Their route lay through a jungle of underbrush and through swamps and streams. They hacked a pathway and waded hip deep through water. Almost four days were spent in covering twenty leagues from St. Augustine to the vicinity of Fort Caroline. In the morning darkness of September 20th, the force camped at a small pond, exhausted, wet and hungry. About the break of day, Menendez assembled his men at the shores of the pond to decide whether to attack Caroline or return to St. Augustine and leave Florida to the French.[2]

The decision was then made to attack the fort that morning, in the midst of a raging storm.

Meanwhile, the French had also been making plans—plans that soon proved to be disastrous. Jean Ribault, having learned that Menendez was in the area, had left with a force of 300 men to go south to search out the Spanish ships and destroy them before they destroyed the French. Before departing, Ribault had once again put

The Destruction of Fort Caroline

the fort under the command of Rene de Laudonniere. We again quote from Mr. Bennett:

> The Frenchmen at Fort Caroline were taken by surprise. Although Laudonniere had ordered watchmen to remain on guard, the incessant rain and wind convinced them there could be no danger of an attack by the Spaniards from distant St. Augustine. The few sentinels who remained at their posts were quickly silenced: Most of the people left by Ribault at Caroline were not experienced soldiers, and many of the fighting men lay ill. Laudonniere himself was sick; so sick, in fact, that he had placed La Vigne, the chaplain, in charge of the sentinels and the latter had dismissed most of the guards because of the bad weather and had gone to bed himself. [3]

Finding the fort almost defenseless, the Spanish easily killed the few sentinels still on duty and entered in to carry out a massacre.

> In less than an hour the Spaniards won a complete victory, with only one of their men a casualty. Many men and some women and children ... were slain in the battle. Some reports of the attack imply that Menendez was a bit tardy in ordering his men to spare the women and children and state that the bodies of some infants were impaled on pikes stuck in the ground. The rest of the women and children were spared.... The other men were hanged ... and the inscription placed over their dangling bodies read, "I do this, not as to Frenchmen but as to Lutherans." Probably as many as 143 Frenchmen were killed or hanged at Fort Caroline. [4]

The fort was then looted for booty to be taken to St. Augustine. All Protestant Bibles and symbols of the Huguenot faith were burned or broken. Finally, Menendez renamed the fort and the river San Mateo, thus removing all vestiges of the French infiltration from the map of La Florida.

The Martyrs of Matanzas

Before we leave the story of Fort Caroline (for there were two other massacres that followed this one) we should mention that there were survivors from this slaughter and one of them was Rene de Laudonniere. Again, quoting:

> On his flight, Laudonniere met Nicolas Le Challeux, an old carpenter and lay preacher who had been amazed by his own ability to leap over the fort's wall and save himself from death. He credited his unusual strength to God. The strong religious beliefs of the Huguenots are illustrated by Le Challeux's account of his escape.
>
> One of our number... proposed... would it not be better to fall into the hands of men than into the jaws of wild beasts or die of hunger in a strange land? I pointed out ... we should be cowards to trust in men rather than in God who gives 'life to his own in the midst, of death, and gives ordinarily his assistance when the hopes of men entirely fail.
>
> I also brought to their minds examples from Scripture, instancing Joseph, Daniel, Elias and the other... and apostles... who were all drawn out of much affliction, as would appear by means extraordinarily and strange to the reason and judgment of men. His arm, said I, is not shortened, nor in anywise enfeebled; His power is always the same.
>
> While thus discoursing, six of the company... abandoned us to go and yield themselves up to our enemies, hoping to find favor before them. But they learned, immediately and by experience, what folly it is to trust more in men than in the promises of the Lord... They were at once killed and massacred and then drawn to the banks of the river, where the others killed at the fort lay in heaps... 5

The Destruction of Fort Caroline

In all, between 50 and 60 Frenchmen escaped from the Spaniards. They left La Florida in two ships bound for France on September 25, 1565.

1 Castillo de San Marcos, Century Souvenir Co., St. Augustine, Fl., 1992 pg. 1

2 Charles E. Bennett, Fort Caroline and Its Leader, The University Press of Florida, Gainesville, FL; 1976, pg. 37

3 Ibid., pg. 37 4 Ibid., pg. 38

5 Ibid., pp. 39-40

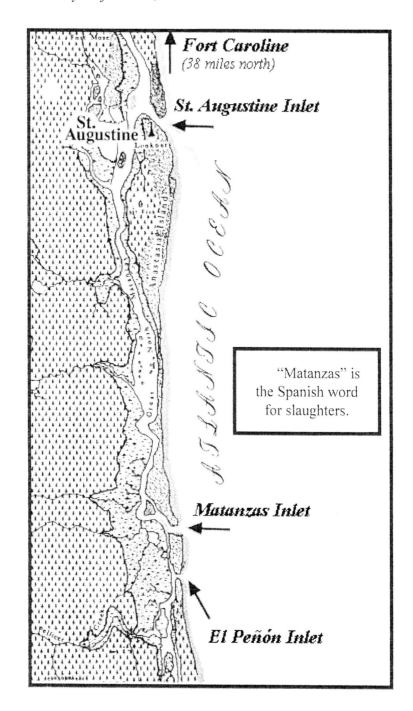

Chapter Three

THE MARTYRS OF MATANZAS

Matanzas: The First Massacre

Menendez returned to St. Augustine, pleased with his efforts at Fort Caroline, but not yet fully satisfied with his mission. His primary goal had yet to be achieved: to find and kill Jean Ribault, the leader of the Huguenot community. Aware that Ribault and 300 of his men had sailed southward down the coast, Menendez' next step was clear—continue to search until those men were found and dealt with.

Ribault, meanwhile, had fallen onto very bad times. Soon after they had left Fort Caroline, Ribault's men, (who were sailing in the three ships), encountered the same storm that had been raging at Fort Caroline. This ferocious hurricane was huge, howling for days up and down the Florida coast. After battling this storm for several days, all three ships were eventually destroyed in the ocean waters, while the men swam to the safety of the shore. They ended up stranded on a strip of sand about fifteen miles south of St. Augustine. There they waited for help while they tried to evade Menendez' search party.

On September 27th, Captain Menendez got the news he was waiting for from the local Timucuan Indians: Ribault and his men had been shipwrecked to the south. They were marching up the coast with several hundred men in two groups, toward Fort Caroline. Menendez then set out with 50 of his men to find them and get rid of them. Two days later, on September 29th, the Spanish met the first group of French on the sands of MATANZAS. It was there that this group had stopped, unable to traverse the deep, running waters of this inlet.

The Martyrs of Matanzas

We now quote from literature provided by the National Park Service:

> Famished and weary, informed of their fort's capture, and tricked into believing the Spanish force to be much larger, the French surrendered. On September 29 they were ferried ten at a time across the inlet, fed and led behind the dunes where their hands were bound. About 200 feet down the beach, Menendez drew a line in the sand.1

At the line, Menendez gave each man an opportunity to renounce his Huguenot faith (called "the new religion") and live, or cross the line and meet his Maker. ***On that day, 111 Christian men chose, as an act of conscience, to cross that line. These were the first martyrs of Matanzas.*** Others would soon follow. Menendez spared only those who stated that they were of the Catholic faith and those who played the flute, timbrel and harp.

Matanzas: The Second Massacre

Even with these two slaughters behind him, Menendez was not satisfied, because Jean Ribault was still alive somewhere on the Florida coast. Again, quoting the Park Service:

> Twelve days later, on October 11, Menendez heard that the second group of 350 Frenchmen had likewise halted at the inlet. Again there was a parley, this time with Ribault himself, who saw the gruesome evidence of the first massacre. (The others had been run through with pike, dagger and sword). Ribault returned and told his men everything. He advised surrender, for he believed it appeared that the Spaniards would show mercy. But during the night, more than half of his men fled south. The next morning, October 12, Ribault and his remaining men handed their battle flags to Menendez.

The Martyrs of Matanzas

As before, the Huguenots were brought in groups of ten across the water and again the white sands were darkened with blood. That day, 134 Frenchmen lost their lives. Sixteen were spared. Later, Menendez sought out those who had fled. Most he took to Habana as prisoners.2

Concerning the exact circumstances of the death of the Huguenot leader, Jean Ribault, we quote from Mr. Bennett:

The man who actually killed Ribault first inquired of him whether the French commander did expect his soldiers to obey orders. Ribault answered, "Yes."

Then the Spaniard said, "I propose to obey the orders of my commander also. I am ordered to kill you."

The Scripture that Ribault recited before the dagger was thrust into his body was Psalm 132, which begins, "Lord, remember David ..." but Ribault began it, according to an eye witness, with "Lord, remember me."3

A Covenant with Zion

When Jean Ribault uttered his last words on the land, as he was being speared through, his words were a prayer from Psalm 132: (Personalized)

Lord, remember me, and all my afflictions: How I swear unto the LORD, and vowed unto the mighty God of Jacob; Surely I will not come into the tabernacle of my house, nor go up into my bed; I will not give sleep to mine eyes, or slumber to mine eyelids, Until I find out a place for the LORD, an habitation for the mighty God of Jacob. (Psalm 132:1-5)

Clearly, the heartcry of this Huguenot leader was to devote his life to establishing "an habitation for the mighty God of Jacob." As Jean Ribault lay dying in the sands of Matanzas inlet that day, 440 years ago, his sacrifice established our land as a permanent "place for the Lord." May we never forget this legacy, as we remain in covenant relationship today with Zion – the land of the mighty God of Jacob.

The Martyrs of Matanzas

Summary

The second massacre of the Huguenots on the sands of Matanzas Inlet marked the end of the brief history of French colonization in La Florida. But this is only the beginning of a more profound story, for the death of the Matanzas martyrs has left a legacy in this country that, until now, has been either largely unknown or ignored.

What is this legacy? Consider the promise of the Word of God in Revelation 12:11: "They overcame him through the blood of the Lamb and the word of their testimony and they LOVED NOT THEIR LIVES UNTO THE DEATH." The martyrs of Matanzas chose death as an act of conscience rather than to bow to the false gospel of Rome. Because they did so at the time of the very (hidden) foundation of our nation, this act of self-sacrifice is one on which our whole nation now rests.

When Pedro Menendez drew the line in the sand against Jean Ribault, the Lord Himself drew a line in the sand against Satan. God's ultimate destiny and purpose for this nation is to function as ONE NATION UNDER GOD and to release the gospel to the uttermost parts of the earth. It will be fulfilled. No weapon formed against us will prosper because of this blood-washed line in the sand. This is America's hidden treasure.

---

1 Fort Matanzas National Monument, Century Souvenir Co., St. Augustine, Fl., 1995, pg. 5
2 Ibid., pg. 5
3 Bennett, Op. Cit. pp. 42-43

TIMELINE OF EVENTS

Attempted Huguenot Colonization of Florida

Easter 1513	Juan Ponce de Leon claims La Florida for Spain
May 1, 1562	Jean Ribault places a marker for France on St. Johns Bluff at the River of May, in present-day Jacksonville Florida.
June 30, 1564	Rene de Loudonniere lands at St. John's Bluff with 300 Huguenot settlers. La Caroline is established.
August 15, 1565	Captain General Pedro Menendez de Aviles leaves Puerto Rico with five vessels.
August 28, 1565	Ribault arrives at Fort Caroline with 600 reinforcements.
September 4, 1565	Menendez discovers Ribault's ships.
September 8, 1565	Menendez moves south and establishes St. Augustine.

Timeline of Events

September 19, 1565   Menendez camps out at Spanish Pond and plans his attack on Fort Caroline.

September 20, 1565   Menendez takes Fort Caroline in a predawn attack; 143 Frenchmen are killed. Some women and children are spared. Laudonniere and a handful of others escapes.

September 29, 1565   Menendez carries out the first massacre at Matanzas; 111 Frenchmen are killed.

October 12, 1565   Second massacre at Matanzas; 134 killed, including Jean Ribault.

November 15, 1565   Laudonniere returns to Europe, with the other survivors. He then writes *The Notable History of Florida*.

The Martyrs of Matanzas

> COMMEMORATIVE TABLET TO THE LIFE OF GASPARD DE COLIGNY
>
> NATIONAL CATHEDRAL: WASHINGTON, D.C.
>
> (Located at the Entrance to the Chapel of St. Joseph of Arimethea)
>
> In Commemoration of Admiral Gaspard de Coligny
>
> Born at Chatillon-sur-Loing, 16 February, 1517
> Assassinated in Paris on the Eve of the St. Bartholomew's Day Massacre
> 24 August 1572
>
> And in Honor of the Huguenots of France Who Died as Martyrs
> In the Cause of Religious Freedom
>
> "I will freely forget all things, whether evil or injury, done unto me alone, Provided that the Glory of God and the public weal by safe."
>
> Admiral de Coligny
>
> MCMXXXIX

Plaque inside National Cathedral, honoring Admiral Gaspard de Coligny, the Huguenot financier who raised funds for the French exploration and colonization of "La Floride" in 1562 and 1564. Coligny was martyred for his faith, in France in 1572.

BIBLIOGRAPHY

*Bennett, Charles E. 1976. Fort Caroline and Its Leader. Gainesville, FL. The University Presses of Florida.

Castillo de San Marcos. (No date) National Park Service. U.S. Department of the Interior.

Castillo de San Marcos. 1992. Century Souvenir Company. St. Augustine. FL.

Claimants for the First Thanksgiving. Plimouth-on-the-Web (Plimoth Plantation's Web Site) http://www.plimoth.org/Library/Thanksgiving/alternat.htm

Fort Caroline. (No date) National Park Service. U.S. Department of the Interior.

Fort Matanzas National Monument. 1995. Century Souvenir Company. St. Augustine. FL.

Laudonniere, Rene. 2001. Three Voyages. (Translated by Charles E. Bennett) Tuscaloosa, AL. The University of Alabama Press.

Manucy, Albert. 1992., Menendez. Pineapple Press, Inc. Sarasota, FL.

Shrine of Our Lady of La Leche. Mision de Nombre de Dios. (pamphlet) (No date) St. Augustine, FL.

Vollbrecht, John L. 1995 St. Augustine's Historical Heritage. C.F. Hamblen, Inc. St. Augustine, FL.

Watson, Colonel James Tompkins. 1908. The Journal of the American History. Experiences of the French Huguenots in America: The King's Refugees. "http://pagesprodigv.com/vrh210a/ressegui/htm"

*Please note: This item is now available only through the National Park Service. Order from Fort Caroline National Memorial, 12713 Fort Caroline Road, Jacksonville, FL 32225. Item #2-1814. $3.95 𝑻

To order copies of
America's First Martyrs go to
www.accentdigitalpublishing.com

Accent Digital Publishing
2932 Churn Creek Road
Redding, CA 96002
530-223-0202
accentdigital@gmail.com

To contact
Sara Ballenger
for presentations on this material
email - ammonet2@patriot.net